D0117148

BABY SLEEP
SCIENCE GUIDE

BABY SLEEP
SCIENCE GUIDE

overcoming the four-month sleep regression

Erin Flynn-Evans, PhD, MPH and
Meg Casano, BSN, MA

Sleep books can be dense and overwhelming.
We designed these guides to be concise
so that tired parents who are short on
time can still read every word.

ISBN: 1532839049
ISBN 13: 9781532839047

Please read all sections carefully.
This book does not constitute medical advice. Check with your child's pediatrician before beginning a sleep plan.

Contents

Introduction

Welcome to the first *Baby Sleep Science Guide* on overcoming the four-month sleep regression. We are Meg and Erin, cofounders of Baby Sleep Science: Sleep Resource Center, a popular online website, blog, and sleep consulting business. Our work is based on current research and practice in the area of infant and toddler sleep. We feel passionately about our mission to help parents improve their children's sleep in a way that feels right to them, by both using science-based knowledge about infant and child sleep and acknowledging and respecting the strong attachments and associations babies develop.

One of the things we love best about our job is speaking personally to thousands of parents from all over the world. The new perspectives, struggles, and challenges families bring to us each day are astounding, thought provoking, and sometimes heart wrenching. We truly enjoy getting to know each family we work with, and for this reason, we know that each family is unique and that there truly is more than one right way to solve your child's sleep troubles.

Over the years, we have come to realize that this particular topic (the four-month sleep regression) is one of the biggest struggles for new parents. The commonly seen increase in night waking around age three to four months occurs at a time when many parents may be heading back to work after a leave and at a time when parents are mentally anticipating infant sleep patterns to be *progressing*, not *regressing*. When the four-month regression hits, it can hit hard and feel so deflating to parents who are already experiencing a deep exhaustion unlike anything they have faced before.

Perhaps more importantly, this is a topic about which so much misinformation as well as inaccurate and downright terrible advice is dispensed to tired new parents and—unfortunately—often by self-proclaimed "certified" sleep consultants. It is for these reasons we chose to start with this subject in our first book, in hopes of reaching as many parents as possible with accurate, sound, and age-appropriate advice for their new babies.

This book is purposely short, yet dense, with loads of information and actionable advice. You'll move through three sections of this book: learning about the problem, evaluating your situation, and—most importantly—solving it, too. There may be times when this book sounds scientific, even a bit clinical, but rest assured—we are moms, too! We know how hard you are trying, how you second-guess yourself, and how those deep, dark hours of the night can be so painful. However, we also know how magical, beautiful, and joyful this time of your life can be, too. We hope this book leaves you feeling hopeful that you can implement change and empowered to do it in a way that feels right for your family.

Step One

Sleep troubles come in many forms, but the four-month sleep regression can be easily distinguished from other issues if you know what to look for. First, you'll need to start by learning these two essential sleep basics:

Sleep Is Important

It's important for growth and learning, emotion regulation, immune function, and for adults, even marriage and relationships. Sleep fragmentation is normal for a little while, and most parents understand it's part of the job. It's lovely to snuggle, nurse, or rock your baby to sleep, and this is a perfectly normal and natural part of parenting. Some parents will prefer always to nurse, comfort, and rock their babies to sleep despite the increased waking that comes with the four-month regression. Other parents will start to feel incredible sleep deprivation—and notice that their babies seem unrested, too—and will work on the changes we describe in this guide. Our goal is to help you work toward age-appropriate expectations using what we know about both the science of infant sleep and the strong associations infants develop to the means by which their sleep occurs.

Newborn Sleep Patterns

Newborns wake only when they are done sleeping or when they have a competing need, such as hunger, discomfort, or needing a diaper change. In most cases, sleep will gradually extend from just a few consecutive hours in each sleep session to long stretches at night with one- to two-hour naps during the day. Some lucky parents will even have babies who start sleeping eight to nine hours "through the night" within the first three months.

Around the third or fourth month, everything changes, and parents may find that their babies who once spent six to nine hours asleep at night are now waking every one to two!

Although most people call this the "four-month regression," it is not really a regression at all. It should be called the "four-month sleep maturation," because a maturing of sleep that occurs between three and five months leads to this change. As babies grow, their sleep grows with them. Sleep changes from a constant state, described above, to a dynamic pattern that includes light sleep (stages one and two), deep sleep (stages three and four, a.k.a. slow-wave sleep), rapid eye movement (REM) sleep, and "checking" wake-ups. These sleep stages are distinct from one another, and understanding them will help you understand why your baby responds differently during various times of the night and day.

STAGES OF SLEEP AND SLEEP CYCLES

Stage One

Stage one is light sleep. It happens for only a few minutes each night. It's the transition from wake to sleep and is marked by heavy or fluttering eyelids and slow, rolling eye movements. If you try to transition your baby from your arms to the crib while she's in stage one, she'll probably wake right up unless she is comfortable getting herself to sleep.

Stage Two

Stage two is also light sleep. About half of your baby's sleep is stage-two sleep, which comprises a little bit of every sleep cycle. Stage two dominates the middle third of the night. An interesting fact about stage-two sleep is that when your baby hears a noise, her brain waves will respond, but she might not fully wake up.

Slow-Wave Sleep (Stages Three and Four)

Slow-wave sleep is deep sleep. Deep sleep dominates the first third of the night, which is why that tends to be the most predictable sleep stretch of the night. During this sleep stage, the arousal threshold is high, so it takes a lot to wake a baby. When your baby does wake from deep sleep, her cries will usually be intense, and she may seem disoriented. During deep sleep, all of your baby's neurons fire in synchrony.

REM Sleep

Rapid eye movement (REM) sleep is light sleep, but it is distinct from the other stages of light sleep. REM sleep dominates the final third of the night. REM is dreaming sleep. It is called "rapid eye movement" sleep because in adults only the upper facial muscles move; the rest of the body is paralyzed so that we don't act out our dreams. Babies don't have REM paralysis and *do* move with their dreams. This means that they laugh, cry, suck, and move during sleep. Be careful not to inadvertently wake your baby during REM sleep. Sleep during the last third of the night is the last to mature, so you may find that your baby doesn't sleep in a predictably sound state during REM sleep until she's six months from her due date.

"CHECKING" WAKE-UPS

Checking wake-ups are the part of sleep that begins after the four-month sleep maturation. These wake-ups happen every sixty to ninety minutes during the night and every thirty to forty-five minutes during the day. We call them "checking wake-ups" because they allow your baby to periodically wake up and check her environment to ensure that everything is safe.

SLEEP CYCLES

During the four-month sleep maturation, the sleep stages described above form sleep cycles. Each sleep cycle is followed by a checking wake-up. A sleep cycle at the beginning of the night might last seventy-five minutes and include fifty minutes of deep, slow-wave sleep and twenty-five minutes of stage-two sleep. A sleep cycle in the middle of the night might include fifty minutes of stage-two sleep, ten minutes of deep sleep, and fifteen minutes of REM sleep. A sleep cycle at the end of the night might include sixty minutes of REM sleep and fifteen minutes of stage-two sleep. A nap sleep cycle might last thirty minutes and include two to three minutes of stage-one sleep, twenty minutes of REM sleep, and seven to eight minutes of stage-two sleep.

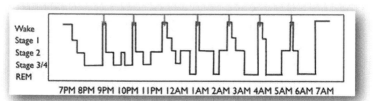

Figure 1. Hypnogram of a mature baby sleep pattern. Sleep typically begins with a transition to stage-one (light) sleep and then progresses to primarily stages three and four (deep) sleep during the first three sleep cycles. As deep sleep subsides, stage-two (light) sleep emerges. At the end of the night, REM (dreaming) sleep dominates. Brief bouts of wakefulness happen at the end of every sleep cycle (indicated in red).

SLEEP ASSOCIATIONS: THE UNDERLYING CAUSE OF FREQUENT WAKING

Now that you know the basics about how your baby's sleep has changed and matured with the four-month sleep maturation, it's time to learn about the practical implications of several parenting responses that can lead to trouble.

Sleeping independently is a learned behavior, but we often don't think about it that way. We are all born with the ability to sleep, but the way we learn to sleep is something that develops in the first few months. We need sleep associations in order to fall asleep. Sleep associations can be simple cues, such as lying in your bed, relaxing your body, slowing your breathing, and closing your eyes. Or, they can involve more complicated rituals.

We expect our sleep associations to remain constant all night. For example, as an adult, you lay in your bed and you fall asleep there with no problem. Although adults also have checking wake-ups every sixty to ninety minutes, you probably don't get up and investigate your surroundings throughout the night. This is because you are established in your sleep space. You are used to your bed, and you feel safe there. However, if you were watching a movie on your couch and accidentally fell asleep there, you probably wouldn't stay asleep. Once you hit one of your checking wake-ups, you would wake fully, recognize you were in the wrong place, and get up and go to bed. If you think about that, it doesn't make a lot of sense. Your couch is probably pretty comfortable, and it's no less safe than your bedroom, yet you would be very unlikely to spend the entire night there. Why? Because it's not the place you identify as the right place for sleep. Your couch is not your sleep association.

Before the four-month sleep maturation, most healthy babies who are free of colic, reflux, or severe allergies are pretty flexible sleepers. Although they don't have a predictable schedule yet, they can usually fall asleep just about anywhere and stay asleep for long stretches of time. As the four-month sleep maturation develops, babies form an identity with their sleep location.

If your baby falls asleep for the night in your arms after feeding, bouncing, or rocking, then she'll be surprised if she wakes up later in the crib. Remember, she fell asleep in your arms, so that's where she thinks she should be for sleep. This means that she has the potential to wake up every sixty to ninety minutes at each checking wake-up! After the four-month sleep maturation, when checking wake-ups begin, this can become a major source of sleep deprivation for families.

You may wonder how your baby can transfer to the crib at all if she thinks that being in your arms is the right place to sleep. Recall that deep sleep happens first, so when you transfer your baby from your arms to the crib at bedtime, it's unlikely she even realizes that you are transferring her. It won't be until she hits her first checking wake-up that she'll come to awareness about her surroundings having changed. If you are lucky, deep sleep will help her stay asleep for two or three sleep cycles (perhaps the first few hours of the night), but when she transitions to lighter sleep, then you'll hear from her. Her cries will tell you that she's tired and confused and in the wrong place for sleep. After you respond to her and replicate the conditions that she experienced when she fell asleep, then she'll be able to go back to sleep. Since sleep gets lighter and lighter as the night goes on, it's typically harder and harder to transfer a sleeping baby back to the crib without triggering an instant waking.

FEEDING ASSOCIATIONS: MORE COMPLICATED THAN OTHER SLEEP ASSOCIATIONS

Feeding to sleep is a sleep association, but it's a bit more complicated than other sleep associations, because feeding your baby also involves some amount of caloric exchange.

Around the same time as the four-month sleep maturation, babies become much more alert. Their visual acuity, gross motor skills, and attention improve, and they become interested in everything. This often leads to distraction during daytime feedings and increased hunger at night. When your baby wakes between sleep cycles at night (now more frequently), you'll probably do as you usually do and feed him back to sleep. As a result, the checking wake-ups described above now take on a dual nature. This doesn't mean that your baby needs to eat more at night in the long term; it just means that he has rebalanced his caloric intake from day to night. If this happens, then your baby doesn't just have a sleep association that can be fixed with learning how to fall asleep on his own; he also has a feeding association that requires that his caloric intake be rebalanced in order for him to consolidate his sleep (sleep longer stretches) again.

You'll learn more about this in the "SOLVE" section below.

CIRCADIAN RHYTHMS AND HOMEOSTATIC PRESSURE: USING THE TWO SLEEP DRIVES TO YOUR ADVANTAGE

We hope you understand how sleep cycles, sleep stages, and sleep associations have contributed to the four-month sleep regression. Before you can solve your child's problem, it's also important to understand *when* you should work on your solution.

There are two sleep drives: homeostatic sleep pressure and the circadian rhythm. Understanding these two sleep drives is important, because when they work in synchrony, your baby will have an easier time falling asleep, and it's the ideal time to start solving a problem. When these two sleep drives are out of sync, your child may exhibit signs of exhaustion and overtiredness but may not be able to sleep. This is not a good time to solve a problem. The following paragraphs will help you understand how to put your baby on a biologically appropriate schedule that will be the most helpful for making improvements.

Homeostatic Sleep Pressure: Avoiding Overtiredness
Sleep pressure is the accumulation of sleep need over time. Sleep pressure is the primary sleep drive during the first few months, and it is the primary determinate of naptime. You will learn that your baby has only a limited window of time when he can stay awake in good form before he needs to sleep again. If your child is taking thirty- to forty-five-minute naps during the day, then he will probably be able to tolerate only sixty to ninety minutes of wake time between sleep

episodes before his sleep pressure builds to a point at which he becomes overtired. As he starts to take longer naps, lasting one to two hours, he'll be able to stay awake for two, even three, hours at a time. As he continues to grow, his ability to tolerate sleep pressure will grow with him, and he'll drop naps and stay awake for even longer stretches of time. It is important that your baby has enough sleep pressure at bedtime to help him sustain a nice, long night of sleep but not so much that he is in an extremely overtired state.

The Circadian Rhythm: Darkness Is Essential

The circadian rhythm is your internal biological clock; it controls the timing of many events in your baby's body, including the drive to sleep and wake. The circadian rhythm is not intuitive. Your child's circadian rhythm is synchronized with the twenty-four-hour day through light exposure. Every morning, when your baby is exposed to light, her circadian clock receives the light signal through her eyes and "sets the clock" to start the day. This means that if your baby has a regular wake time, with regular morning light exposure, her internal clock will be predictable. If she is exposed to light at varying times each day, then all of her internal timing will be off, and it will be difficult to know when your child is ready for sleep. The circadian rhythm is responsible for setting your child's biological bedtime and her biological wake time.

In order to set your child's circadian rhythm, you'll need to keep it very dark at night (even in the early morning) when you want her to be able to sleep, and you'll need to make sure she is exposed to light beginning at a consistent time each morning.

Your baby's sleep timing can be changed. The circadian rhythm resets every day, so if you want your baby to have a different schedule than what she is currently on, you can help her adjust by controlling her exposure to light and darkness. For example, shifting her schedule later would include gradually increasing light exposure in the evening while increasing darkness exposure in the morning. The circadian rhythm does not shift quickly; it takes about three days following a new light-dark cycle for your baby's body to respond.

The interaction between sleep pressure and the circadian rhythm is complex. The circadian rhythm also controls the drive to be awake, and the strongest drive to be awake happens right before your child's biological bedtime. This window of time is called the "wake-maintenance zone" (WMZ, or the "second wind").

During the wake-maintenance zone, it is very hard for your child to sleep. For example, if your baby's biological bedtime is eight o'clock at night, but you try to put her down at seven, she may show very strong sleepy signs—especially if she missed a nap—but may not be able to sleep. This is because the wake-maintenance zone may prevent her from being able to sleep, even if she is very tired from insufficient napping. The consequence of this is that from seven to eight in the evening, you may have a very fussy, tired baby who just can't fall asleep.

For this reason, it's important to keep daytime sleep adequate while trying to solve a problem related to the four-month regression. We discuss nap strategies in the coming paragraphs.

SCHEDULE AND FEEDING EXPECTATIONS

NIGHTS

By four months old, your baby's bedtime should be regular, happening within the same thirty-minute window most of the time. If your baby is having age-appropriate naps as described in the "Naps" section (below), he will usually be awake for two to three hours between his last nap and bedtime.

If you do not already have a regular bedtime for your baby, try to spend four to five nights working on that. Pay attention to the timing of the last nap as it relates to bedtime. In some cases, you may need to try very hard to help your baby nap at the end of the day so he can make it to your goal bedtime without too much overtiredness. Other times, less commonly, you may need to wake your baby from a too-long nap in the early evening so that he's tired enough at his regular bedtime. Of course, it's always OK to put your baby to bed earlier than planned if he missed a nap altogether. We do not suggest forcing your young baby into very long stretches of wakefulness at this age.

Most babies have the capacity to sleep for ten to twelve hours (with one or two feedings) overnight at four months. The average sleep duration for night sleep at this age is ten and a half to eleven hours of sleep. Babies with shorter naps and two or more night feedings tend to need a longer time in bed. Babies with longer naps and/or no night feedings tend to need a shorter time in bed at night. Please take a moment to assess your night sleep length expectations. It is unlikely your four-month-old baby will sleep more than a total of fourteen to fifteen hours in a twenty-four-hour period so be sure to add up daytime sleep as well.

FEEDINGS

It is reasonable for most babies to go through the entire ten- to twelve-hour night with one or two feedings at four months. Your baby's weight is just one part of the equation; your child's metabolism, feeding history, growth rate, your desire to breastfeed, and history of medical conditions like reflux all come into play when determining an appropriate number of night feedings. It is always a good idea to check with your pediatrician about how many feedings your baby needs, because every baby is different. It is not considered a sleep problem if your baby is eating twice a night at four months old.

NAPS

Unlike night sleep, short, single-sleep-cycle naps are typical between four and six months of age. Many young babies are not able to take naps lasting more

than thirty to forty minutes without additional soothing from their caregivers. Babies at this age need
about three to four hours of daytime sleep, so your
baby could take as many as three to six naps in a day
until she gets closer to six months. Short, thirty- to
forty-minute naps will likely happen every one to one
and a half hours. Longer, one- to two-hour, naps will
likely happen every two or more hours.

Although most parents would prefer to have their
babies sleep sixty to ninety-plus minutes in a row at
predictable times, these short naps are developmen-
tally normal, and even a very restrictive napping intervention isn't likely to lead to a predictable clock-time
nap schedule at this point in your baby's life. For this
reason, it may be necessary for you to assist your baby
with napping as you begin working on night sleep. It
is important that your baby maintain adequate daytime sleep as you work on change overnight.

You may be able to help your baby extend naps during the day by soothing, holding, or bouncing him if
he wakes after about thirty to forty minutes. You may
also find success in anticipating your baby's waking
and offering some soothing before he's awake from
his single-sleep-cycle nap. This is encouraged when
possible. Sleep tends to become more difficult as the

day wears on, so taking a walk, wearing your baby in a soft carrier, or having some snuggle nursing may be helpful in obtaining those late-day naps.

Now is simply the time to lay a solid foundation for your baby to grow into naps by promoting a good sleep environment and keeping your baby well rested.

Step Two

Before you move to the "SOLVE" section of this guide, you'll need to evaluate your baby's current sleep pattern:

- Evaluate your baby's sleep environment and presleep routine using the worksheet provided below. The environment should be cool, very dark, and quiet, with nothing changing (turning on or off) all night.
- Figure out your baby's biological bedtime and wake time and how much awake time she can tolerate between naps. (If your baby's bedtime is seven o'clock, but she is rarely asleep before eight, despite rocking, feeding, and holding, you'd consider her bedtime eight o'clock as you embark on change in the next section.)

- To help with this, use the sleep log provided below to track the time your baby falls asleep each night for four to five days and formulate an achievable goal. You'll need to make sure your baby is ready for sleep when you are asking her to sleep.
- Make adjustments to ensure that her bedtimes and morning wake times are regular each day (within the same thirty-minute window) and that naps are within the normal range for her age. It is OK to shift her bedtime earlier from time to time when needed in the event of daytime sleep loss or overtiredness.
- Provide soothing or comfort as needed to help your baby nap or to help extend daytime naps and keep your baby rested. Make informed choices, and follow the safety guidelines of the AAP.
- Determine how many night feedings your baby needs based on the information provided in the "Schedule and Feeding Expectations" section (above), and write it in the worksheet provided below.
- Determine what sleep association your baby requires to get back to sleep. Does your baby need to nurse? Have a bottle? Pacifier replacement? Rocking? Bouncing?

SLEEP SCHEDULE AND ENVIRONMENT WORKSHEET

Use this worksheet to create a solid sleep foundation for your baby before beginning any intervention. Share this document with other caregivers so your child has the consistency that is so important to long-term success.

Schedule

Our child's target bedtime: _____

_____

Our child's target wake time: _____

_____

Our child's target nap times: _____

_____

Our child's target night-feeding times: _____

_____

What we will do to achieve this schedule:

While implementing the plan to maintain consistency, some things we may need to do differently:

Presleep Routine

In the ten minutes before every nap, we will:

In the fifteen to thirty minutes before bedtime, we will:

SLEEP-ENVIRONMENT CHECKLIST

- Remove excessively bright or blue/green night-lights.
- Turn off light sources on baby monitors, humidifiers, etc.
- If desired, install a dim red or amber-colored nightlight for safety or comfort.
- Black out your child's room so that the transition from night to day is not obvious.
- Turn on lights at a regular time in the morning. Keep it dark before that time.
- Consider a continuous white-noise machine at a comfortable volume near the source of erratic noises, for example, near a window or door to block out dog barking, doorbell ringing, or creaky floorboards.
- Turn off all music and variable sounds (such as bird or whale songs) before placing your baby in bed.
- Ensure that the ambient temperature in your baby's room is below seventy-two degrees.
- Dress your baby in breathable fabric appropriate to the season. Skin should not be sweaty or icy cold.

- Remove all loose items from your baby's sleep space for safety (no blankets, pillows, stuffed animals, etc.).
- Consider using a humidifier during the winter in dry environments (clean it regularly).

PRESLEEP CHECKLIST

- Crib/sleep environment is safe and prepared according to AAP guidelines.
- Baby is wearing comfortable clothing for sleep.
- Feet are covered with socks, footie pajamas, or a sleep sack/wearable blanket.
- Baby is clean and dry.
- Baby has been fed within thirty minutes of going to sleep at bedtime, or will not be hungry and due to eat in the middle of a naptime.
- Perform a bedtime routine lasting five to fifteen minutes before a nap and fifteen to thirty minutes before evening bedtime.
  - Include elements that you and your baby enjoy and that you can repeat each night, such as changing clothes, massaging or therapeutic touching, singing or playing soft music, swaying, bouncing, snuggling, reading a story, or looking at photos.

SLEEP-ASSESSMENT CHART

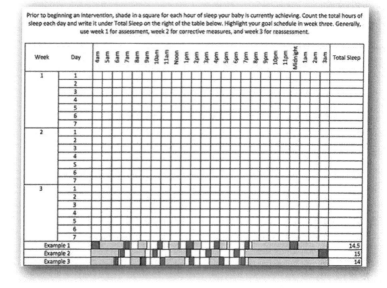

In the examples above, gray shading represents sleep, and green shading represents feedings. These sample schedules will not work for every baby or family. They are provided to help you see different typical schedules. As you work through your plan, you should adjust your baby's sleep timing to suit his or her individual needs and the needs of your family while, overall, working on a regular bedtime and wake time each day. Some babies may be eating more or less than the feeding schedules depicted on the graph above. Consult with your pediatrician before eliminating feedings.

Example One: *Two-Feeding Night* Babies who need two feedings at night will often spend eleven to twelve hours in bed at night, with a feeding around four to six hours after going to bed and another spaced three to four hours after that. Babies with shorter naps often need more nighttime sleep. This example shows three hours of total napping. Note: The feeding before bed would optimally be timed at the beginning of the bedtime routine, not at the end.

Example Two: *One-Feeding Night* Babies who need just one feeding a night typically spend ten and a half to eleven hours in bed at night, with a feeding around seven to eight hours after going to bed. Total naptime is usually three to four hours in this scenario. Note: The feeding before bed would optimally be timed at the beginning of the bedtime routine, not at the end.

Example Three: *No Night Feedings* Babies who no longer need to eat at night usually have a shorter night of sleep, lasting around ten to eleven hours. Napping typically totals around three and a half to four hours. Note: The feeding before bed would optimally be timed at the beginning of the bedtime routine, not at the end.

Step Three

Now that you have the foundational pieces in place, the next step is to teach your baby how to sleep independently. The rationale is this: *when your baby has checking wake-ups during the night that are unrelated to hunger, the crib will feel like a safe and reasonable place in which to go back to sleep (without needing you).*

If your baby has a feed-to-sleep association and is eating more than one to two times at night, then you will need to evaluate her hunger and feeding needs as your first step. If your baby has a rocking/bouncing/swaddle/pacifier or similar sleep association, then you can skip the feeding section and select an intervention strategy below.

IF YOUR BABY HAS A FEED-TO-SLEEP ASSOCIATION

If your baby always falls asleep while eating, it may be very difficult to offer any other form of soothing during the night (such as rocking, patting, or bouncing) as you respond with your sleep intervention of choice. For babies with a feed-to-sleep association, it is often helpful to establish a *new* sleep association (such as bouncing, rocking, or pacing around the room) first. Then, you can more easily use this new sleep association to help your baby adapt to consolidated sleep in a crib or bassinet.

To do this, feed your baby approximately thirty minutes before bedtime with the lights on and in a room that your baby does not associate with falling asleep. Then, continue with the rest of your bedtime routine. Instead of having feeding be the very last thing before bed, add an additional step or two such as turning on a fan or white-noise machine, swaying, shushing, or singing a lullaby (this will become your new bedtime routine, so choose things you enjoy doing). Stay in your baby's room and rock, comfort, or pace with her until she falls asleep instead of having her fall asleep at the breast or bottle. For babies with nurse-to-sleep associations, it may be helpful to have the nonnursing parent take the lead on this comforting for the first few nights.

If feeding is a very strong association, your baby may feel frustrated by this change and cry, so you can kiss, snuggle, and comfort him through this adjustment, right in your arms. Your goal is not to put him into the crib awake just yet; it's simply to help your baby learn to fall asleep in a new way, without eating. It may take thirty to sixty minutes for him to fall asleep in your arms on the first night. You can then transfer your sleeping baby into his place of sleep. If he pops up again forty minutes later, return to rock/soothe/bounce him in the same way you did at bedtime.

Within three to five nights, your baby should adapt to the new routine and accept your comforts as the new way to go to sleep at bedtime.

EXTRA NIGHT-WAKING—IS SHE/HE HUNGRY?

You certainly don't want to deny your baby feedings when he is hungry, so it can be really difficult to disentangle true feeding needs from sleep associations. Still, it can be done if you pay close attention to your baby's pattern. If your baby had been sleeping from seven-thirty at night until one in the morning, eating, and then sleeping from one to four in the morning, eating, and then sleeping until six in the morning, then you have a good sense of his true needs. If one day somewhere around the three-to-four-month mark, he's up at one in the morning *and* at two-thirty, yet perfectly healthy, you can begin to suspect that this might be the beginning of the regression. If your baby hasn't suddenly increased daytime feeding (which might indicate a growth spurt), then it's probably the regression creeping in on you. Since you can feel pretty confident that your baby doesn't need to eat at both one and two-thirty in the morning, this would be a good time to teach your baby to go back to sleep in new ways. For example, feed him at one o'clock as usual. Then at two-thirty, simply rock, bounce, or hold him (using the strategies you started at bedtime to transition away from a feed-to-sleep association) until he goes back to sleep, rather than feeding him. The goal is to keep his nighttime caloric intake stable, while at the same time teaching him that there isn't just one way to fall asleep. The rocking can also become a sleep association, so if your baby continues to wake up and isn't hungry but wants to be rocked to sleep, you'll learn how to solve that problem below.

REDUCING EXTRA NIGHT-FEEDINGS

The steps described in the section above (using rocking or other comforting to soothe through extra, non-feeding waking) work great for babies who were on a regular feeding pattern *before* the regression and who have started waking more frequently, but whose parents have not yet started feeding them more frequently.

When the four-month-regression waking starts, parents often interpret these new instances of waking not as sleep maturation but as hunger, and they start doing what they usually do when their babies wake: feed them! So then you end up with a flip-flop of calories where your baby may be taking in more calories at night than during the day. Even a small increase in nighttime caloric intake can become habitual. Although your baby doesn't *need* to eat every ninety minutes, if you have gotten into the habit of feeding him that often, his little tummy will think he does. You don't want to stop cold turkey any feedings involving caloric exchange.

Is your baby now eating a lot more at night than he was before the regression?

Is he eating a lot less during the day?

If the answer is yes to either or both of these questions, then you need to taper his feedings at night before doing anything else and increase his calories during the day.

To do this, first determine what times he needs to eat. Typically, the first feeding happens after four to six hours (e.g., around twelve or one in the morning), and the second feeding happens about three to four hours later (e.g., three or four in the morning). If your baby is now eating at ten at night, twelve-thirty, two-thirty, and five in the morning, you'll plan to eliminate gradually the feedings at ten at night and two-thirty in the morning.

Figure out how long he eats during his one or two extra feedings overnight (or how many ounces he's taking if bottle-feeding) and just work on reducing his extra feedings a little each night by reducing minutes nursed or ounces in a bottle. As you reduce each extra feeding, rock/bounce/hold your baby with the same soothing you practiced at bedtime. Plan to keep one to two feedings overnight.

During the day, make sure you feed your baby in a quiet, distraction-free environment in order to ensure he gets nice full feedings. Consider cluster feeding at the end of the day so he has had ample opportunity to eat as bedtime approaches. Plan to spend about one week rebalancing caloric intake in this manner (reducing extra feedings slowly overnight and increasing them during the day).

Once he's just eating a tiny bit or for a very short duration during those extra instances of nighttime waking, you can start rocking or soothing him (using the soothing you established at bedtime) through the extra waking instances rather than offering a feeding.

Within a week, your baby may still be waking frequently for some rocking or soothing, but feeding to sleep will only be happening at one or two needed times overnight, and you now have a clearer picture of your baby's nighttime feeding needs.

All of this important prep work and background has led you to the point where you are now able to ask your baby to get back to sleeping those long stretches at night again!

SLEEP INTERVENTIONS

Every baby and family is different, and there is no one-size-fits-all approach to teaching your baby to sleep independently. We have listed four different sleep interventions below, in no particular order, to help you accomplish this goal. Although we sometimes recommend less interactive approaches than those outlined here, due to the young age of babies during the four-month sleep maturation, most of these options involve you or your partner staying in the room or frequently interacting with your baby.

These strategies are appropriate for babies who are four to five months from due date and should be used *only at bedtime and during the first half of the night to start*. Before six months of age, your baby's sleep is likely immature during the second half of the night; thus sleep interventions may be unsuccessful at that time.

You should not use these strategies at a time when your baby is hungry. Use the strategies described above to guide your baby into a predictable nighttime feeding pattern first.

One or two of the strategies may or may not appeal to you for a variety of reasons. Choose the approach below that best fits your parenting style and family needs. When considering which approach to choose, do not pick a strategy that you cannot implement consistently during the first half of the night. Repeatedly starting and stopping any strategy typically leads to worse sleep problems. Do not begin any intervention until you are absolutely ready to start.

Do not mix and match strategies. Do not begin a strategy if your baby is sick.

For babies between four and six months old, either use these strategies at bedtime only to just get the hang of things *or* at bedtime and for any nonfeeding waking between the hours of bedtime and approximately twelve to one in the morning. For example, if you weaned away a ten o'clock feeding and replaced it with rocking, you may use your intervention at both bedtime and ten o'clock now.

Reread the section on daytime napping if needed. It is very important that your baby is napping adequately as you begin to work on nighttime sleep.

Style One: Baby-Led Intervention

Best for: families who are not in crisis mode and who may simply be looking to work on small changes with their newborns. Also good for parents who do not wish to leave their babies alone and prefer a very slow, gradual, and interactive progress.

How long will it take? Approximately two to four weeks (or more). Clear and obvious improvements should be apparent within just one or two weeks, but due to potential schedule changes as your baby grows, illness, or travel, the overall scope of the plan may take more than one month.

What to do:
Step One:
Prepare your baby for bed at his usual bedtime, and ensure he's had good feedings close to bedtime. If you just changed a feed-to-sleep association as described above, you'll want to use the new sleep association to soothe your baby at the end of your bedtime routine.

Step Two:
When your baby appears tired but is still awake and aware of his surroundings, put him in his sleep space.

Step Three:
As you do this, continue to stand close to, or lean over, the bassinet/crib/sleep location and pat, shush, and/or

hum to your baby from close by after placing him/her down awake.

Step Four:
At first this might feel a little confusing to your baby, and if he begins to get upset or distressed in any way, you'll pick him up and repeat your sleep cue (lullaby, rocking, swaying, bouncing, etc.), but then be sure to put your baby down awake to try this new experience again.

Step Five:
Depending on your motivation and your baby's level of sleep pressure, you can rock/bounce/soothe him to sleep in your usual way after just a few practice runs in the crib, *or* you can continue to try this until he falls asleep in the crib with your soothing. With this particular method, you may wish to repeat this many times in a row but should stop these attempts if you or your baby becomes very cranky or overtired.

The goal of this particular style is to keep your baby happy and comfortable with the crib/sleep location and to increase the exposure to the crib very slowly over time.

Step Six:
Continue to offer these brief crib exposures each evening at bedtime, with frequent soothing breaks whenever needed. With time, your baby will become more and more comfortable with the crib. You may also use this technique in the first half of the night for any additional pop ups (e.g., forty minutes after bedtime, or ten o'clock) if you have weaned down feedings at those times. Do not do this at a time when your baby is hungry.

Once your baby is comfortable falling asleep in the crib, you may move on to "exiting the room" steps from other interventions below.

This is a baby-led strategy, so you will introduce change incrementally at your baby's pace. With this particular plan, you would not "make" your baby stay in the crib when he is crying. If you are unsuccessful at transferring him into his crib without crying at first, it's OK. Rock him to sleep instead, and continue practicing the development of this skill on subsequent nights. Look for signs of progress every three to five nights. If your baby's pace is too gradual for you, then consider one of the parent-led approaches below.

Style Two: Parent-Led Interventions

Option Two-A: Repeated Sleep Cues: In the Room
Best for: parents who wish to stay in the room with their babies and provide lots of interaction and cuddles as they work toward change yet who wish for a faster timeline than with a baby-led intervention.

How long will it take? Approximately two weeks.
You should see obvious change within three to five nights. Expect your baby to be comfortable falling asleep in the crib with soothing by the end of one week. Expect one additional week to work on exiting the room and completing your plan.

What to do:
This strategy involves two phases: teaching your baby to fall asleep in the crib with your help and teaching your baby to fall asleep in the crib without your help. Each phase will take at least three to five days to reach initial success.

Phase One
Step One:
Start your baby's bedtime routine and soothing about fifteen minutes later than you typically do. This will

help increase sleep pressure without making your baby too overtired.

Feed and then soothe your baby as you learned about in the sections above, and then place your baby in the crib or bassinet while he is still awake and aware of where he's going.

Step Two:
After placing your baby in the crib awake, stand at the side of the crib and offer some soothing such as patting, shushing, or rubbing. Offer this soothing for one minute.

After one minute, if your baby is upset, pick your baby up and provide your baby with the sleep cue that you used to end your bedtime routine. For example, if you swayed with your baby while singing a song as the last step in your bedtime routine, repeat that song and swaying now as a way to re-cue your baby to sleep. This sleep cue may last about one minute and *should not* last long enough to put your baby to sleep.

Step Three:
After the sleep cue, put him back down into the crib awake. He may begin to fuss.

Let him spend two minutes in the crib while you resume patting, soft shushing, and verbally consoling him.

After he spends two minutes in the crib, pick him up and repeat your sleep cue for no more than one minute.

Step Four:
Place your baby back in the crib awake, and pat, shush, and verbally console him while he is in the crib. Let him spend three minutes in the crib.

Pick him up and repeat your sleep cue for one minute.

Continue this pattern, always putting your baby down awake after soothing. Increase the time your baby spends in the crib until you reach five minutes. Pick your baby up and repeat the sleep cue every five minutes thereafter.

If you are working on nonfeeding night waking in the first half of the night, then use the same scheme for night waking, beginning with a one-minute waiting period.

Each night, repeat the same process of putting your baby down awake and picking him up to take snuggle breaks, but increase the time he spends in his crib.

How many minutes you wait isn't as important as increasing your waiting times each night. As an example, on night two, wait two minutes, then three minutes, then four minutes, then five minutes, and then every six minutes. On night three, wait three minutes, then four minutes, then five minutes, then six minutes, and then every seven minutes, and so forth.

Progress isn't always apparent night to night, but the general trend should be improvement. By night five, your baby should accept having you soothe him at the cribside and should require few sleep cues.

During the night, feed your baby at the times you identified. Always keep your intervention separate from feeding. If your baby wakes at a time when you aren't sure if he's hungry or not, then feed him. You can then use your intervention to ask him to go back to sleep independently. *It is very important to avoid beginning a series of sleep cues followed by feeding.* If you are asking him to go to sleep in the crib, then you should continue your intervention until he falls asleep. If it is time for him to eat, then he shouldn't have to wait; you should go to him and feed him right away.

Do not switch off between caregivers within a single transition to sleep. It can be very stimulating and frustrating to see one parent and then the other. It is OK for multiple caregivers to participate in the plan, but each person should follow through with the intervention until your child falls asleep. At the next wakeup, the other caregiver can take over.

It will likely take about thirty to sixty minutes for your baby to fall asleep during each of the first four nights, because he will have no idea what he is supposed to do or how to fall asleep on his own. After three to five nights of falling asleep in the crib, he will begin to associate your sleep cues with going to sleep. He should be able to fall asleep within about twenty minutes at bedtime on night five.

Optional Components:

It is OK for a parent to sleep in the room with the baby during this phase.

It is OK for one parent to take charge of most/all of the night waking.

It is OK to start this strategy for bedtime only for the first three or four nights.

Phase Two

When your baby becomes receptive to your cribside soothing and is falling asleep in the crib without feeding or rocking to sleep, it's time to work on exiting the room altogether. If you chose to start with this strategy, now proceed to the next option.

Option Two-B: Repeated Sleep Cues: Out of the Room

Best for: parents who wish for a fast-paced plan that still includes snuggle breaks, yet who prefer the option to step out of the room for brief periods as they work toward change with their babies.

How long will it take? Approximately ten days. Obvious change should be apparent within three to five nights. Total plan duration is approximately seven to ten nights.

What to do:

Step One:

Start your baby's bedtime routine fifteen minutes later than you usually do to maximize sleep pressure without causing overtiredness. Be sure your baby has had a day of good feedings and a good feeding within the last half hour before your goal bedtime. Perform your baby's bedtime routine and soothing and place her in her crib when she is still awake.

Step Two:
After placing your baby in the crib awake, step out of the room. Stay out of the room for approximately one minute. If, after that one minute, your baby is crying or unhappy, return to your baby and take a soothing break using the rocking/bouncing/holding you learned about in previous sections.

Step Three:
When you have finished soothing, place your baby in the crib awake again and leave the room. Wait outside of the room for two minutes.

Then, return to your baby and take a snuggle break using the same soothing as before, always making sure you put her down awake to try again.

When you have finished soothing, leave again. Wait three minutes.

Just as with Option Two-A, "Repeated Sleep Cues: In the Room," continue increasing the intervals by one minute until she falls asleep. It will likely take about thirty to sixty minutes for her to fall asleep the first night.

Exiting the Room

Each night, repeat the same sequence of putting your baby down awake and leaving the room, but increase the time you spend out of the room.

For example: on night two, you may wish to leave the room for two minutes, then four minutes, then six minutes, then eight minutes, and so forth, until she falls asleep. On night three, you may start with five minutes, then seven minutes, then nine minutes, and so forth.

Progress isn't always apparent night to night, but the general trend should be improvement, and by night five to seven, your baby should be falling asleep much more quickly with you out of the room.

In the night, continue to feed your baby at her one or two needed feeding times.

Option Two-C: Uniform Response: In the Room
Best for: parents who wish for a fast-paced plan with few rules and quick results but who are uncomfortable leaving their babies alone.

How long will it take? Approximately one week.
Obvious change should be apparent within three to four nights. Total plan is complete within approximately one week.

What to do:
Step One:
Start your baby's bedtime routine fifteen minutes later than you normally do to maximize sleep pressure without causing overtiredness. Be sure your baby has had a day of good feedings and a good feeding close to bedtime. Perform your baby's bedtime routine and soothing, and place your baby in the crib when your baby is still awake.

Step Two:
Sit, stand, or kneel close to your baby's crib, and wait with him until he falls asleep. You may shush, hum, or whisper from time to time so he knows you are there with him and that he is not alone. You may offer pats or rubs from time to time, too, but you should stop patting or rubbing before your baby is asleep. Wait with your baby until he falls asleep (approximately forty to sixty minutes in most cases) and then leave the room.

Step Three:
Repeat this same response for the next three to five nights. Your baby should become accepting of your presence of soothing by the end of three to five nights.

Exiting the Room

Typically, with this type of strategy, when your baby is able to fall asleep in the crib with minimal cribside responses from you, it becomes quite easy to walk out of the room after a soothing bedtime routine. If it seems difficult to exit the room, you may follow the steps from Option Two-B, "Repeated Sleep Cues: Out of the Room," to complete your plan.

Conclusion

We like to think of your path to improving your child's sleep as a bit like a choose-your-own-adventure story. Your family is unique, and so is your baby. You will make choices based on your present life circumstances, past experiences, and perhaps, from the way you were parented. The choices you make for one child may not be the same as those you make for another.

Remember that you have all the tools you need right here to start making progress overcoming the four-month regression right away. Think about the big topics we covered in the "LEARN," "EVALUATE," and "SOLVE" sections, and double-check your baby's sleep environment and safety as well as your expectations for night sleep and total sleep in a twenty-four-hour period. Determine how many feedings your baby needs overnight and if you will be reducing any night feedings. Make a choice about the pacifier or swaddles (see Addendum). Finally, think about the method that feels like the best fit for your family as you begin to teach your baby the process of falling asleep, and then implement it with consistency.

Try to keep the big picture in mind as you work through change by watching for your baby to make progress every several days rather than within individual nights. Use the Sleep-Assessment Chart to track your progress, and try to evaluate information from a few days in a row rather than micromanaging each individual nap or moment overnight.

If you feel uncertain or just need some cheerleading, you can always ask us a question on our business Facebook page, Baby Sleep Science: Sleep Resource Center, or come to our website, www.babysleepscience.com, and browse our library of free blogs and webinars on dozens of popular infant and toddler sleep topics. And, of course, you are always welcome to schedule an appointment to talk to one of us personally.

We hope you learned something new from our book and that you and your baby are on the path to improved sleep already!

Take care,
Meg and Erin

Addendum

A Special Note about Pacifiers, Swaddles, and Sleep Suits

HOW DOES THE PACIFIER FIT IN?

We have a comprehensive blog on pacifiers and pacifier use from newborns to age four located on our website at www.babysleepscience.com. We include an overview below.

Make informed choices. The AAP recommends using a pacifier in the first year as one factor (of which there are many) in the reduction of SIDS.

Like nursing or bottle-feeding to sleep, the pacifier is a sucking-to-sleep association that may lead to sleep-cycle wake-ups all night. You'll have the best results if you stop sleep associations that require you, the caregivers, to be involved. If you'd like to continue to use the pacifier during the four-month regression, you will always have to help your baby find it when he needs it, since he is not old enough to do it on his own. Your baby will typically be old enough to find it himself around seven months of age.

If your baby cannot find the pacifier without your help, and you cannot continue to replace it as often as you have been, due to your own severe sleep deprivation, stop using it at bedtime. You may continue to use the pacifier during the second half of the night, when sleep is still immature, as described in the "LEARN" section. You may continue to use the pacifier during the day to preserve daytime naps as you work on your nighttime plan.

SWADDLES AND SLEEP SUITS: NOT A ONE-SIZE-FITS-ALL ANSWER

It may be best, before beginning sleep training at this age, to discontinue the use of swaddles and sleep suits and switch instead to a sleep sack, if appropriate for your baby's room temperature. Your baby will then have access to her hands and arms in order to position herself comfortably or to find her fingers, thumb, or pacifier (if older) for self-soothing while you are working through your plan.

However, for some four-month-olds, the startle reflex is still strongly present, and hands and fingers are most definitely *not* soothing. Use your judgment. If your baby is not yet rolling, and you think your baby will do better with arms out, then discontinue the swaddle at bedtime. Discontinuing the swaddle may be done slowly over a one- or two-week preparatory phase by stopping first at bedtime and soothing your baby in a new way—such as rocking or holding—in tandem with changing a feed-to-sleep association as described in the first paragraph of the "SOLVE" section. You may need to continue to swaddle your baby after the first nighttime feeding or night wake-up and gradually reduce the amount of time spent in the swaddle over several days or weeks. If it is safe (i.e., your baby is not rolling), *you may continue to swaddle your baby for nap sleep* to help maintain naps, even though you may be discontinuing it at night.

If you think your baby will be far more bothered by flailing hands and scratching fingernails, you may wish to keep your baby in a swaddle or sleep suit at this young age—as long as your baby is not rolling.

70834620R00042

Made in the USA
San Bernardino, CA
08 March 2018